Roasts & Toasts

Snappy One-Liners for Every Occasion

GENE PERRET
with Terry Perret Martin

Illustrated by Myron Miller

Sterling Publishing Co., Inc.
New York

Edited by Jeanette Green

Library of Congress Cataloging-in-Publication Data
Perret, Gene.
    Roasts & toasts : snappy one-liners for every occasion / Gene
Perret ; with Terry Perret Martin ; illustrated by Myron Miller.
        p.   cm.
    Includes index.
    ISBN 0-8069-9444-4
    1. American wit and humor.   I. Martin, Terry Perret.   II. Title.
PN6162.P396   1997
818'.5402—dc21   96-37008

3   5   7   9   10   8   6   4

Published by Sterling Publishing Company, Inc.
387 Park Avenue South, New York, N.Y. 10016
© 1997 by Gene Perret and Terry Perret Martin
Distributed in Canada by Sterling Publishing
% Canadian Manda Group, One Atlantic Avenue, Suite 105
Toronto, Ontario, Canada M6K 3E7
Distributed in Great Britain and Europe by Cassell PLC
Wellington House, 125 Strand, London WC2R 0BB, England
Distributed in Australia by Capricorn Link (Australia) Pty Ltd.
P.O. Box 6651, Baulkham Hills, Business Centre, NSW 2153, Australia
Manufactured in the United States of America

Sterling ISBN 0-8069-9444-4

For my Sophia
      —Grandpop

For Little Miss Sophia
      —Mommy

For consistency and simplicity, the authors used male pronouns where there was a choice throughout this book. Readers, though, can easily adapt most of the jokes to apply to either men or women.

CONTENTS

LET THE ROAST BEGIN

We gather here in friendship. A toast to good friends: Each time you become one, you gain one.

A toast to friendship: Not all of us can love our enemies, but we can all treat our friends a little better.

When our journey through this lifetime ends, the richest are those with many friends.

Here's to our toastmaster for the evening: A toastmaster is a person who eats a meal he doesn't want so he can get up and tell a lot of stories he doesn't remember to people who've already heard them.
—*George Jessel*

IRREVERENT INTRODUCTIONS

Why don't the feller who says, "I'm not a speechmaker," let it go at that instead of giving a demonstration? —*Kin Hubbard*

A speech is like a love affair. Any fool can start it, but to end it requires considerable skill. —*Lord Mancroft*

He hasn't got much to say, but at least he doesn't try to say anything else. —*Robert Benchley*

Here's a speaker who needs no introduction. Believe me, we've tried several and they don't help.

• • •

You've heard of many speakers who need no introduction. Here's a speaker who doesn't deserve one.

• • •

Let's bring our next speaker on with a great big hand. It may be the only one he gets all night.

. . .

I could say many nice things about our next speaker, but I'd rather be honest.

. . .

You're in for a special treat tonight. Our next speaker has promised to keep it short.

. . .

This next gentleman is not a professional speaker and you'll have the opportunity this evening to see why.

. . .

There are some speakers who need no introduction. But our next speaker needs all the help he can get.

. . .

Our next speaker is one who keeps listeners on the edge of their seat. What happens is many of them doze off and slide forward.

. . .

Our next speaker is a man who has received so many accolades that he finally had to look the word up in the dictionary.

. . .

I've heard it said about our next speaker that no matter what you pay him, he's worth every penny of it. He's speaking here tonight for free.

. . . So don't get your hopes up.

. . .

Our next speaker needs no introduction—especially not the ridiculously inflated one that he wrote here.

. . .

What can I say about our next speaker . . . that wouldn't make us look foolish for bringing him here?

. . .

What can I say about our next speaker that he probably hasn't already said about himself?

. . .

And now our final speaker of the evening. You've often heard the expression "last but not least." Tonight is the exception to that rule.

. . .

Our next speaker not only needs no introduction, it probably wouldn't do any good.

. . .

We searched high and low for an interesting speaker for this evening. We found our next speaker during the low part of the search.

. . .

This gentleman is one of the most sought-after speakers in the country. But enough about his outstanding bench warrants.

. . .

Many of you have heard our next speaker before. We appreciate your sacrifice in being here anyway.

. . .

People on our committee said, "We want an entertaining speaker. Get (*name of speaker*)." I said to them, "Make up your minds."

. . .

It's not easy finding entertaining and enlightening speakers for these events. So now I'd like to present to you, straight from the bottom of the barrel . . .

. . .

I talked to members of other associations and they were delighted that we had booked this next speaker for our meeting. It meant that their group didn't have to book him.

. . .

As you all know, we don't pay our speakers much. I'm happy to say this next gentleman is worth every penny of it.

. . .

I always look for one outstanding trait to feature when introducing a speaker. So, please welcome a speaker now who fits into our price range.

AFTER A BAD INTRODUCTION

I could stand up here and be very funny, but I don't want to change the format of your show.
—*Jack E. Leonard*

I've always wanted to be one of those speakers who needs no introduction—especially after receiving one like that.

. . .

When I was a kid I had a puppy dog who ran away. That had always been the worst day of my life . . . until tonight's introduction.

. . .

I don't know whether I've just been introduced or read my Miranda rights.

. . .

I've never received an introduction like that before. And if my lawyer is worth his salt, I'll never receive one like that again.

. . .

Thank you, I'm happy to be here . . . having survived that introduction.

. . .

Thank you. I'm happy to be here. After that introduction, I'm happy to be anywhere.

. . .

Thank you. I must tell you, I've received much worse introductions than that . . . and from much better people.

. . .

Unfortunately for me, that was a terrible introduction. Unfortunately for you, it was appropriate for my presentation.

. . .

When people ask me, "Who would you like to introduce you?" I generally say, "Oh anybody." After this evening I'm going to say, "Oh, anybody except . . ."

. . .

I'm always worried that the introduction is going to make promises to the audience that I, as a speaker, cannot live up to. No problem with that tonight.

. . .

[*Name of introducer*] talked to me earlier and said, "What would you like me to say in your introduction?" I said, "Use your own good judgment." That's the last time I'll make that mistake.

. . .

I thought that was a very creative and funny introduction. I can't wait to call my attorney to see if he agrees with me.

AFTER A GOOD INTRODUCTION

What a wonderful introduction. I just hope it doesn't put me into a higher tax bracket.
—*Bob Hope*

That was a wonderful introduction. Now even I can't wait to hear what I say.

. . .

That's a fantastic introduction. If I had known I was that good, I would have charged more.

. . .

That's probably the best introduction I've ever received in my whole life—except for one time when the host said, "Why don't you just stand up and introduce yourself."

. . .

I wish my parents could have heard that glorious introduction. My Dad would have been so proud. And my Mom, God bless her, would have probably believed most of it.

. . .

That was a terrific introduction. In fact, in the middle of it, I turned to the person next to me and said, "Who is he talking about?"

". . . I'd like to meet the guy."

. . .

That was a very eloquent introduction. The problem is: it was so well done, now it's going to make my speech look bad.

. . .

I've always believed the best introduction was just to tell the simple truth about a person. But I liked this much better.

. . .

That introduction was very flattering. When I go to meet my Maker, could you come along with me?

. . .

That's the most flattering introduction I've ever received. And you read it just the way I wrote it.

. . .

That was a very gracious introduction. In fact, I'm sorry I have to speak now. I'd rather sit here all night and listen to your introduction.

. . .

Boy, if I had known I was going to get such a magnificent introduction, I would have brought along a better speech.

THE GUEST OF HONOR'S FAMILY

You know, you have very beautiful children. It's a good thing your wife cheats.
—*Joey Bishop*

We don't want our guest of honor's family to be shocked by some of the things we say tonight. We're only kidding. Besides, a lot of the nice things we say about him aren't true, either.

. . .

Our guest of honor has his entire family here with him tonight. You know how hard it is to get a baby-sitter once the children get into their twenties.

. . .

Right here, at the beginning of the program, I'd like to introduce the members of our guest of honor's family. By the time we get done with him, they may no longer want to be associated with him.

. . .

As you can see, our guest of honor is very fortunate to have such charming children, none of whom look like him.

. . .

Our guest of honor has his entire family with him tonight. But that's not going to stop us. We've still got them outnumbered.

. . .

We invited our guest of honor's family to be here with him tonight. We had to have someone sit at his table.

. . .

I'd like to warn our guest of honor's family that we are going to do a lot of bad jokes about him. We don't do it because we want to. It's just that with him, it's so easy.

. . .

I spoke with one of our guest of honor's sons before the dinner. He told me he always wanted to grow up to be just like his Dad. I think tonight may change his mind.

. . .

Our guest of honor wanted to have his family with him tonight—as character witnesses.

. . .

Our guest of honor's family is here tonight, but they know him as a husband and a father. They don't know him as a working man. Come to think of it, neither do we.

. . .

Our guest of honor is a husband, a father, and to us, a coworker. I'm sure he's a wonderful husband and father. And two out of three is not bad.

. . .

I spoke to a member of our guest of honor's family before the banquet. He said, "I know this is a roast, but go easy on my Dad." I want the entire family to understand that no matter how cruel the jokes may sound, no matter how vicious the insults may seem, in your father's case, we are still going easy.

THE GUEST OF HONOR

They never give you a dinner—until you don't need one.
—*Will Rogers*

I think the world of you . . . and you know what I think of the world.
—*Henny Youngman*

15

We've had fun with our guest of honor tonight. And he sat there patiently while his wife explained the jokes to him.

. . .

Tradition dictates that we give our guest of honor the last word. However, tradition has no idea how dull he is.

. . .

Our speakers this evening have tried to be clever, funny, and entertaining. Now it's our guest of honor's turn. Unfortunately he's none of those things.

. . .

We've had a lot of fun here tonight. Now for a change of pace, I introduce our guest of honor.

. . .

We've taken great liberties with our guest of honor tonight. We've kidded him, taunted him, insulted him, but we feel we can do it with a guy like him because he has very little idea of what's going on.

. . .

We're now going to give our guest of honor equal time. But because he's such a dull guy, it will seem much longer.

. . .

I'll give you an idea of what kind of guy our guest of honor is. I leaned over to him a minute ago and said, "We're now going to give you a chance to respond to all of this." He said to me, "You mean they've been talking about me all night?"

. . .

Right now I'd like to introduce a prince of a guy, a hard worker, a great personality. I'd like to introduce that person, but instead I have to introduce our guest of honor.

. . .

I'd like to introduce a person now who has been a real good sport throughout this entire evening. Either that or he has absolutely no concept of what's going on.

. . .

We've had a lot of fun here tonight, but all good things must come to an end. With that in mind, I introduce our guest of honor.

. . .

We've said a lot of silly things this evening. We've poked fun, we've exaggerated. Now it's our guest of honor's turn to stand up and show you that we weren't that far off.

. . .

We've poked a lot of fun at our guest of honor tonight, but deep down inside we know that we didn't do half the stuff we could have. Now it's his turn.

. . .

I've been to a lot of these roasts and I've heard merciless jokes told about a lot of people, but I can truthfully say that never before have I seen a guest of honor who was so worthy of them.

. . . Here he is now to show you what I mean.

CELEBRATING

OUR GUEST OF HONOR

Dislikes People

Refuses Advice

Is Opinionated

Is a Procrastinator

Is an Optimist

Is a Pessimist

Is Absent-Minded

Needs Some Manners

Could Have Been a Diplomat

To our guest of honor! You've heard the expression "To know him is to love him." Our guest of honor has heard it, too.

Please raise your glasses and drink to our guest of honor. Why? Because it's as good an excuse as any.

We come here tonight to pay homage to our guest of honor. The word *homage* may be a little strong, but he doesn't care because so is what he's been drinking.

To our guest of honor! The nicest thing we can say about him is that he's a friend.

DISLIKES PEOPLE

Why be influenced by a person when you already are one?
—*Martin Mull*

Popularity is the easiest thing in the world to gain and the hardest to hold.
—*Will Rogers*

I like to reminisce with people I don't know. Granted it takes a little longer.
—*Steven Wright*

Nobody liked me because I was too popular.
—*Jackie Vernon*

Our guest of honor feels this way about people: if it weren't for them, we wouldn't have to worry about traffic.

. . . or deodorant.

Our guest of honor just doesn't like people. When he goes to a party, he stays in the room with the coats.

• • •

He has an answering machine that says, "At the sound of the beep, hang up."

. . .

You must admit that people can sometimes be annoying; so, our guest of honor just tries to get in his shots first.

. . .

According to our guest of honor, the world's problems started when Adam and Eve decided to have children.

. . .

He has to learn that people aren't perfect, but they're the best company we've got.

. . .

He learned it from his uncle. His uncle enjoyed being alone so much, he formed the Hermit's Association.

. . . but he was the only one who showed up at the meetings.

. . .

He plans on going to heaven when he dies. He hates crowds.

. . .

It's an interesting philosophical question: If there were no people on earth, would humankind be better or worse off?

. . .

There would be no wars if there were no people. Who would we shoot at?

. . .

He once wanted to form a club for people like himself—the Perfect People's Association. But he sent out the invitations without stamps.

REFUSES ADVICE

I always pass on good advice. It is the only thing to do with it. It is never any use to oneself.
—*Oscar Wilde*

It's better to keep your mouth shut and appear stupid than to open it and remove all doubt.
—*Mark Twain*

It's always a silly thing to give advice, but to give good advice is absolutely fatal.
—*Oscar Wilde*

When I get one of those "mom" headaches, I take the advice on the aspirin bottle. Take two and keep away from children.
—*Roseanne Barr*

Advice is a drug in the market: the supply always exceeds the demands.
—*Josh Billings*

Here's some advice my mother gave me ... trust your husband, adore your husband, and get as much as you can in your own name.
—*Joan Rivers*

Never mind what I told you, do what I tell you.   —*W. C. Fields*

Advice: the smallest current coin.   —*Ambrose Bierce*

When a man comes to me for advice, I find out the kind of advice he wants, and I give it to him.   —*Josh Billings*

Put all your eggs in one basket—and watch that basket.
—*Mark Twain*

Our guest of honor feels about advice that it's truly better to give than to receive.

• • •

The only advice his mother ever gave him was "Don't have children."

. . .

He believes the best things in life are free—except for advice.

. . .

I agree with our guest of honor. I've been suspicious of advice ever since someone who was worse off than me told me how to better myself.

. . .

Our guest of honor believes the only advice to listen to is from wealthy, successful, powerful people. But then, what would they be doing talking to him?

. . .

He claims the best advice he ever got was "Don't listen to advice."

. . . he listened.

. . .

There's good advice and there's bad advice. If you're giving it, it's good; if you're listening to it, it's bad.

. . .

Most people ask for advice because they just want to hear someone else say what they're thinking.

. . .

Good advice is like the bottle of bitters you keep in the bar. It lasts a lifetime because you hardly ever use it.

. . .

Our guest of honor says a piece of advice should be like the common cold. If you've got a good one, keep it to yourself.

. . .

Be careful giving advice to people. It's the only commodity where if it's good, people get mad at you because it wasn't better.

IS OPINIONATED

When I need your opinion, I'll give it to you. —*Sam Levenson*

Public opinion in this country runs like a shower. We have no temperatures between hot and cold. —*Heywood Broun*

Loyalty to petrified opinions never yet broke a chain or freed a human soul. —*Mark Twain*

It is not best that we shall all think alike; it is difference of opinion that makes horse races. —*Mark Twain*

Yes, our guest of honor is opinionated, but if people didn't have different opinions, Baskin-Robbins could have gotten by with just one flavor.

. . .

Our guest of honor has an opinion; you and I have a stupid argument.

. . .

It's important to remember: one doesn't have to think to form an opinion.

. . .

Just because there are two sides to every argument doesn't mean either one is right.

. . .

If people held on to their principles the way they hold on to their opinion, this world would be a better place.

. . .

Opinions are like children. We always think ours are the best.

. . .

Differing opinions can make for an interesting debate, except in hockey, where it usually makes for a five-minute major penalty.

. . .

I've told our guest of honor often: "I respect your opinion. It's you I don't like."

. . .

Our guest of honor is entitled to his own opinion. What bothers him is when people think they're entitled to theirs, too.

. . .

Our guest of honor has already formed his opinion. Please don't distract him now with facts.

. . .

Anyone can have an opinion. Only those who agree with him can have a correct opinion.

. . .

Argument-ender: I will defend to the death your right to have an opinion, but I must warn you—you're getting dangerously close to that point.

IS A PROCRASTINATOR

Do not put off till tomorrow what can be put off till the day after tomorrow just as well.
—*Mark Twain*

Don't put off until tomorrow what you can do today. There may be a tax on it by then.
—*Milton Berle*

My mother said, "You won't amount to anything because you pro-crastinate." I said, "Just wait."
—*Judy Tenuta*

He who hesitates is a fool.
—*Mae West*

Our guest of honor claims he's not a procrastinator, but he hopes to be someday.

. . .

Our guest of honor told his wife, "Don't plan anything for this Fourth of July. I don't want to miss the Procrastinator's Christmas Party again this year."

. . .

In his biography our guest of honor wrote, "I'm definitely a pre-crastinator . . . a procastineater . . . a precrestinater. . . . Someday I'm going to learn how to spell that word."

. . .

Do you know what a nudist is? A person who wears hand-me-downs from a procrastinator.

. . .

Our guest of honor enjoys procrastination. It gives him something to do tomorrow.

. . .

Our guest of honor got good news today from the Procrastinators Society of America. The results of the election are in. He was president last year.

. . .

Our guest of honor is a procrastinator. He was going to quit the Procrastinators Society, but he never got around to it.

. . .

To a procrastinator, *today* is Latin for "my day off."

. . .

The invitations to the Annual Procrastinators Ball, which was held two months ago, were mailed out today.

. . . At the bottom they read, "Please send regrets only if you weren't here."

. . .

I may be a procrastinator or I may not be. I've just never gotten around to looking up that word in the dictionary.

. . .

Our guest of honor has a beautiful sign that reads, "Do it now." But he hasn't hung it up over his desk yet.

IS AN OPTIMIST

Optimist: Day-dreamer more elegantly spelled.   *—Mark Twain*

Definition of an *optimist:* A 94-year-old man who marries a 24-year-old girl and starts looking for a nice home close to a school.
—Woody Woodbury

An optimist is a guy who looks forward to the great scenery on a detour.   *—Milton Berle*

Our guest of honor is an optimist. An optimist is the kind of a person who will believe campaign speeches.

. . . even ones he makes himself.

. . .

An optimist is a person who buys something with a 90-day-warranty and expects it to work perfectly on the 91st day.

. . .

Optimism sees the bright side of everything—even pessimism.

. . .

I don't know what I am. I'd like to be an optimist, but I have a bad feeling about it.

. . .

It's easy to spot an optimist. He's the one wearing sunglasses in a thunderstorm.

. . .

A really great salesman is one who can sell an umbrella to an optimist.

. . .

You show an optimist the dark side of the moon and he'll see the bright side of it.

. . .

An optimist can see the good in everybody. The rest of us just don't have the time to look that hard.

. . .

Optimists are the cheerleaders of life.

. . .

The worst part about arguing with an optimist is, even if you win, he's happy.

. . .

Optimists like happy endings. That's why you'll rarely see a Southern optimist reading a Civil War novel.

Life is divided into the horrible and the miserable.

—*Woody Allen*

Things are going to get a lot worse before they get worse.

—*Lily Tomlin*

I told my psychiatrist that everyone hates me. He said I was being ridiculous—everyone hasn't met me yet. *—Rodney Dangerfield*

Our guest of honor is definitely a pessimist. A pessimist is a guy who would say, "Monday I hit the lottery for $2 million. Tuesday I won $100,000 at the track. Today, nothing."

. . .

A pessimist is a guy who hates all good things because he knows they must come to an end.

. . .

The pessimist and the optimist refused to marry because they couldn't decide how to raise the children.

The optimist was sure they'd turn out to be happy children; the pessimist wasn't sure they'd turn out to be children.

. . .

A pessimist is a person who carries a rabbit's foot to remind him how much luck it brought to the rabbit.

. . .

When things really can't get any worse, a pessimist finds some way to think they can.

. . .

An optimist sees the glass as half-full. The pessimist complains about what it's half-full *of*.

. . .

A pessimist will sit there and curse the darkness rather than light one little candle and then sit there and curse the light.

. . .

Our guest of honor is the kind of guy who, if he goes to a picnic where there are no ants, he thinks it's because the potato salad is no good.

. . .

Our guest of honor is someone who knows the movie is going to be lousy, but he goes anyway because he likes to complain about the popcorn.

. . .

You should always have a pessimist as your best man. That way the bride's parents might be glad she married you.

. . . unless they're both pessimists, too.

IS ABSENT-MINDED

There was an absent-minded professor who saw the sign he put on his door that said, "Back in thirty minutes." So he sat down to wait.
—*Milton Berle*

There are three signs of old age. One is loss of memory. The other two I forget.
—*Bob Hope*

Have you heard the one about the executive who was so old that when he chased his secretary around the desk, he couldn't remember why?
—*Larry Wilde*

Our guest of honor is so absent-minded, on Easter morning he can hide his own eggs.

. . .

Our guest of honor not only forgets names and faces, but the difference between the two.

. . .

Our guest of honor is so absent-minded, at the beginning of each workday he writes his name on a piece of paper. That's so at the middle of the workday, he'll remember who he is.

. . .

Our guest of honor is so absent-minded, he answers every question the same way: "What was the question?"

. . .

He's so forgetful that he's a real slow reader because everytime he turns the page, he forgets why.

. . .

Someone asked our guest of honor to pass the salt and pepper. He said, "Here's the pepper. Now what was that first thing you asked for?"

. . .

At work, we call him "Frothy" because after he brushes his teeth in the morning, he forgets to rinse.

. . .

He makes new friends easily. He has to . . . he can't remember the old ones.

. . .

The company takes advantage of his forgetfulness. He's worked here about thirty years. Management says in five or six more years they'll hold his 25th anniversary party.

. . .

He's very absent-minded. He never makes the same mistake twice . . . as far as he's concerned.

. . .

I asked our guest of honor once when his birthday was. He said, "Sometime this year."

. . .

Our guest of honor has two friends who are just as absent-minded as he is. Their favorite pastime is to get together and then one of them leaves. The other two try to guess which one left.

NEEDS SOME MANNERS

Good breeding consists in concealing how much we think of ourselves and how little we think of the other person.

—*Mark Twain*

It's gotten so that if a man opens a door for a lady to go through first, he's the doorman.

—*Mae West*

He's so polite, his tombstone will read, "Pardon me for not standing."

—*Milton Berle*

He was a gentleman all over; and so was his family. He was well born, as the saying is, and that's worth as much in a man as it is in a horse.

—*Mark Twain*

I'm always a gentleman. Whenever I see an empty seat on a bus, I point it out to a lady. Then I race her for it.

—*Henny Youngman*

Our guest of honor believes that etiquette is for highbrows. If you can't spell it, you don't need it.

• • •

At the kind of restaurants he goes to, the only rule of etiquette is not to tell anyone what's in the secret sauce.

• • •

Our guest of honor's mom said to him at an early age, "Don't you want to learn to be polite and refined?" He said, "No, thank you."

• • •

His brothers and sisters always had good manners at the dinner table—at least until the food fight broke out.

• • •

His mom kept repeating, "Don't put your elbows on the table. Don't put your elbows on the table." He grew up assuming all other parts of the body were OK.

. . .

His table manners are atrocious. I know chicken can be eaten with your fingers, but not when it's in soup.

. . .

My mother always said she wanted her children to act like little ladies and gentlemen, which was confusing for us since we were all boys.

. . .

My mother had a rule at the table: no one could start eating until everyone was served. Some people would call that etiquette; she called it a fair fight.

. . .

My mom would say, "If you don't have good manners how do you ever expect to have dinner at the White House?" I'd say, "I could be elected President."

. . .

My mom always said that good manners were just common sense. But so was getting to the meat loaf before my brother Jimmy got to it.

. . .

At our house, we had another word for good table manners—*starvation*.

. . .

It's always considered bad taste to spell out naughty words with your alphabet soup before eating it.

COULD HAVE BEEN A DIPLOMAT

That's called diplomacy, doing just what you said you wouldn't.
—*Will Rogers*

A diplomat is a man who can convince his wife she looks bad in a mink.
—*Milton Berle*

You can diplomat America out of almost everything she has, but don't try to bluff her.
—*Will Rogers*

To make a good salad is to be a brilliant diplomatist. The problem is entirely the same in both cases. To know exactly how much oil one must put with one's vinegar.
—*Oscar Wilde*

Our guest of honor likes to think of himself as a diplomat. Diplomacy can sometimes be the art of looking someone in the eye and stabbing them in the back at the same time.

. . .

Diplomacy is the art of being able to cut someone's legs out from under them and still leave them standing on their own two feet.

. . .

Diplomacy is the art of giving the other guy exactly what he wants, whether he wants it or not.

. . .

Diplomacy would be like Pinocchio telling a lie and not even having his nose know it.

. . .

33

A diplomat is a salesman with a sash across his chest.

. . .

A diplomat is someone who can tell you good news and bad news, and you can't tell the difference.

. . .

Saying, "No, you can't have that" is dictatorial. Getting the other guy to say, "No, I don't want that" is diplomacy.

. . .

Diplomacy is when you steal from someone, instead of saying, "Stop, thief!" they say, "Thank you."

. . .

Diplomacy is being born with a silver fork in your mouth instead of a forked tongue.

. . .

A diplomat is the only person who can say to an opponent, "Congratulations, you lose."

. . .

A diplomat is the only person who can report to his boss, "I've spoken with the enemy and I think I've got them exactly where they want us."

. . .

Diplomacy is the art of winning without having the other guy lose.

A SPECIAL ROAST FOR

FELLOW WORKERS

The Boss

A Coworker

A Hard Worker

Not a Hard Worker

A Talker

A Party Guy

To my fellow workers:
  We've made some profit.
  We've made some loss.
  We've made them both,
  Despite our boss.

To my fellow workers:
  To those who toil hard in the workplace
  I raise my glass on high.
  To those who gave their all for the company,
  Here's a toast to me and one other guy.

To my fellow workers:
  We work in the trenches
  Day after day.
  Your friendship makes it worthwhile.
  It's certainly not the pay.

THE BOSS

A good executive never puts off until tomorrow what he can get you to do today.   —*Joey Adams*

A good executive is a man who believes in sharing the credit with the man who did the work.   —*Joey Adams*

A vice-president in an advertising agency is a "molehill man"—that's an executive who comes to work at 9 A.M. and finds a molehill on his desk—and by 5 P.M. he makes it into a mountain.   —*Fred Allen*

Everything he touches turns to gold. I'm afraid to go to the toilet with him.   —*Milton Berle*

The boss, what an idiot. I told him how to run the company. We parted good friends, though. He boarded his yacht and I took the subway home.
                                                              —*George Jessel*

This is a new experience for me—saying things about our boss in front of his face.

· · ·

This is a night for all of us to gather together to honor our boss, share a meal and a few drinks with him, and in general, pretend that we like him.

· · ·

They asked me to say a few words about our boss. My mom always taught me if you can't say something nice about a person, don't say anything at all. So, if you'll all join me now in a moment of silence . . .

· · ·

It's easy to say nice things about our boss. About his leadership, his fairness, his understanding. That's easy. The hard part is keeping the straight face.

· · ·

I wanted to say about our boss that he was born to lead, to pull his share of the load, to be a working part of the team. Then it dawned on me that you could say those same things about a Siberian husky.

. . . and they're friendlier.

· · ·

Our boss was never too busy to be sympathetic when we were in trouble. He always gave us a cold shoulder to cry on.

· · ·

I wouldn't say our boss was tough, but periodically he'd go to a palmist to get his brass knuckles read.

· · ·

Our boss was always ready to listen to our troubles. But then, why shouldn't he? He caused most of them.

· · ·

Our boss told us from day one that his door was always open. And it was. It wasn't until recently that we found out that was by order of the fire marshal.

· · ·

I remember our boss philosophizing: "Happiness in life is something to do, someone to love, and something to hope for." Then he'd add, "Now get the hell to work."

. . .

Our boss often told me his secretaries couldn't keep their hands off him. It was true. They all wanted to choke him.

. . .

And our boss is clumsy. He wanted us all to put our best foot forward, but he kept tripping over it.

. . .

Whenever we had troubles that we wanted to discuss with the boss, he'd listen and have those three words that we all came to know: "Like I care."

A COWORKER

She's the kind of girl who climbed the ladder of success wrong by wrong.
—*Mae West*

Someday you'll go far and I hope you'll stay there.
—*Henny Youngman*

There's absolutely nothing our guest of honor wouldn't do for this company and there's absolutely nothing the company wouldn't do for him. That pretty much sums up their relationship. All these years they've done absolutely nothing for each other.

. . .

I've been our guest of honor's best friend for many, many years, and quite frankly, I think it's someone else's turn.

. . .

What do you say about someone whom you've sat next to in the office for so many years. Three words come to mind: "Do some work."

. . .

If you have trouble in the office, you can go to our guest of honor. If you have problems at home, you can talk to him. If you have troubles at any time, you can go to him. Why? Because you know he's not doing anything.

. . .

Our guest of honor is the kind of a guy you want to have working at your side. If the boss drops in unexpectedly you'll always look good by comparison.

. . .

I worked with our guest of honor for many years. And I'll say this, through thick and thin, happy and sad, good times and bad, he'll always be there for you. You know he's not going to get promoted.

. . .

I've recommended our guest of honor for jobs and promotions. In fact, the first day he walked into the office I turned to the boss and said, "Get him."

. . .

Our guest of honor is a good guy to have in the office because he's good for a lot of laughs. Of course, most of them are behind his back. . . .

. . .

As a coworker our guest of honor is unique. There's only one of him which is good because that's all our office can afford to carry.

. . .

Our guest of honor is not only my coworker, but I'd also say he's my best friend. Which should give you an idea of how lousy my social life has been.

. . .

Our guest of honor and I have been together through thick and thin . . . but enough about both of our waistlines. . . .

A HARD WORKER

Every morning I get up and look through the *Forbes* list of the richest people in America. If I'm not there, I go to work.

—*Robert Orben*

He's a self-made man . . . the living proof of the horrors of unskilled labor.

—*Ed Wynn*

He's always got his foot to the pedal, his shoulder to the wheel, his nose to the grindstone. How he gets any work done in that position, I'll never know.

. . .

Many times I've seen our guest of honor at work at the office even when he was sick. I assume he was sick. I'd hate to think anyone could look that bad when he was well.

. . .

I'll say this for our guest of honor: he pulls his own weight, which for him is a considerable amount of work.

. . .

What makes him happy is to have a demanding, challenging project on his desk. It makes the rest of us happy, too, because it keeps him out of our hair.

. . .

I told our guest of honor once that "all work and no play make Jack a dull boy." So now, he and Jack hang around together.

. . .

He's very ambitious. Someone asked him once, "What do you want?" He said honestly, "I want your job." Unfortunately, he was speaking to the janitor at the time.

. . .

Our guest of honor is attracted to work like a bee is to honey, which is annoying to the rest of us because the buzzing keeps us awake all day.

. . . it could also explain why he refers to the rest of us as "drones."

. . .

Our guest of honor is not happy unless he's working. If you don't believe me, take a look at him tonight.

. . .

He's the hardest worker I've ever seen in all my years at my desk. It might also explain why I've been at the same desk all these years.

. . .

Our guest of honor came into our office and worked harder than the rest of us and will probably move ahead of the rest of us. But that's not all. There are many other reasons why we don't like him.

. . .

Our guest of honor works so hard that he makes the rest of us work harder, too. In fact, he works right through lunch. Well, why not? He can't get any of us to eat with him.

NOT A HARD WORKER

The man with the best job in the country is the Vice-President. All he has to do is get up every morning and say, "How's the President?"
—*Will Rogers*

I was a lousy accountant. I always figured that if you came within eight bucks of what you needed you were doing okay. I made up the difference out of my own pocket. —*Bob Newhart*

He has a problem with his job. He doesn't do anything; so, he never knows when he's finished. —*Milton Berle*

There's no limit to the amount of work a man can do, provided, of course, that it isn't the work he's supposed to be doing at that moment. —*Robert Benchley*

The pencil sharpener is about as far as I have ever got in operating a complicated piece of machinery with any success. —*Robert Benchley*

Hard work never killed anybody, but why take a chance? —*Charlie McCarthy*

You know the old saying: If you want something done, give it to a busy man. Well, if you don't want something done, give it to our guest of honor.

. . .

He knows he's not a hard worker. Every payday he comes to work wearing a ski mask.

. . .

He has a sign over his desk that reads, "Thank you for not working."

. . .

Our guest of honor is very, very good at not doing any work. I went with him to the zoo one day. And when we got to the sloths' cage, they all came up and asked for his autograph.

. . .

If our guest of honor left our office it would take three workers to replace him. One to do his job and two to finish up the work he hasn't completed yet.

. . .

He was given a job and the first question he asked was "When do you need this done?" The boss said, "I don't need it done. That's why I gave it to you."

. . .

Our guest of honor has very simple work demands. All he needs is a project to work on and an office that sleeps one.

. . .

At work, our guest of honor keeps his nose to the grindstone and his shoulder to the wheel. The strange thing is, he can sleep in that position.

. . .

His out-basket caught fire once and he didn't discover it for four months.

Now he doesn't even have one. He's such a slow worker that the two baskets on his desk are marked "In" and "Still In."

. . .

Our guest of honor is the only guy I've ever worked with who, when he takes a two-week vacation, his productivity doesn't drop.

. . .

Our guest of honor considers himself a meticulous worker. He does nothing, but he does it without mistakes.

A TALKER

When Mohammed Ali was born, he was a six-pound mouth.
—*Bob Hope*

Jessel likes after-dinner speaking so much, he starts a speech at the mere sight of bread crumbs.
—*Fred Allen*

I finally found out why talk is cheap. There's more supply than demand.
—*Joey Adams*

Our guest of honor is an eloquent conversationalist, which means when he talks, everybody listens ... but nobody knows what he's talking about.

. . .

I asked him. I said, "Don't you agree it's wrong to use a big, complex word when a simple one will do?" He said, "Indubitably."

. . .

Our guest of honor loves to talk. Even when he has nothing to say, he usually says it.

. . .

He has such a big vocabulary I can't really converse with him. The best I can do is nod in all the right places.

. . .

He has such a sophisticated vocabulary he makes William F. Buckley sound like Beavis and Butthead.

. . .

Our guest of honor loves to talk. When you ask him, "How are you doing?" he actually tells you.

. . .

He was born with a silver spoon in his mouth, but he took it out right away because he wanted to say something.

. . .

His parents still remember their first words after he was born: "Shut up."

. . .

Our guest of honor has a very powerful voice. He can call you on the telephone without even using the telephone.

. . .

His telephone voice is so loud, you can hang up on him without losing volume.

. . .

He has a very loud voice. He once called a group of us into his office, and every one went in—even people who weren't at work that day.

. . .

He yelled at me once and it took three weeks for my shoes to stop vibrating.

A PARTY GUY

Our guest of honor is a real party guy. You should see him at a convention . . . because chances are he can't see you.

. . .

Our guest of honor passed out at a party we had not too long ago. So we brought him to . . . then we brought him two more and he was fine.

. . .

Our guest of honor loves a good party. In fact, he loves it so much he often turns it into a *bad* party.

. . .

He loves parties. His middle name is RSVP.

. . .

Our guest of honor loves a good party. And if he has a good time at an affair, the next day we tell him about it.

. . .

His philosophy is "eat, drink, and be merry because the next party may not be for a whole week."

. . .

At one convention he woke up in his hotel room, and his clothes were strewn all over the floor. And he was still in them.

. . .

Our guest of honor likes to have a good time because, he says, life is too short. Of course it's short when you only remember about half of it.

. . .

Our guest of honor says he enjoys parties because he's full of life. I've seen him at some parties where that's not all he was full of.

. . .

Our guest of honor likes to have a good time with good friends. "Although," he says, "sometimes with bad friends you can have an even better time."

. . .

Our guest of honor says he can have a party with just himself and one good friend. In fact, he could have a great party without the one good friend, but then how would he get home?

. . .

I asked his wife earlier if he ever goes to sleep early. She said that he often goes to sleep early—about 50 feet before he reaches the front door.

A TOAST

ON THIS SPECIAL OCCASION

MR. TOAST

SPRONG

25 YR.
PROMO
LEAVING

25 Years with the Company

Promotion

Leaving the Company

I drink to your 25 years with the company. It's amazing how time flies when you're forced to share an office with someone.

A toast: May you sit on the tack of success and rise quickly.

I toast your moving on to bigger and better things. We hated to lose you to another company, but it was the only way we could get rid of you.

25 YEARS WITH THE COMPANY

Our guest of honor is celebrating his 25th anniversary with the company tonight. So many years, so little accomplished.

· · ·

Our guest of honor serving 25 years here makes us proud of ourselves. Not many companies could have endured that so graciously.

· · ·

Twenty-five years is a long time. Those of us who have worked with our guest of honor know that.

· · ·

I asked our guest of honor, "How do you feel about reaching the 25-year mark?" He said, "I feel great. Next I'm going for the quarter century."

Everyone understood that joke except the group from Accounting.

· · ·

Let me give this audience an idea of what 25 years is: Count all your fingers on both hands. Now do it again. Then count the fingers on just one hand.

... For many of you that will come to 25.
... If it doesn't, have a friend count them for you.

· · ·

Our guest of honor reported to this company 25 years ago—bright, eager, wet behind the ears. He's dried up since.

. . . behind the ears and a few other places.

• • •

I think our boss summed up this evening best when he said about our guest of honor, "Twenty-fifth anniversary? I thought I fired him years ago."

PROMOTION

You can sum up his success in one word, *lucky*.   —*Joey Adams*

I don't deserve this award, but I have arthritis and I don't deserve that either.   —*Jack Benny*

Our guest of honor has been promoted. That's great. It means there's hope for all of us.

• • •

Congratulations on your promotion. It couldn't have happened to a nicer person. A lot more deserving maybe, but none nicer.

• • •

The Peter Principle says that workers are promoted until they reach their level of incompetence. This promotion disproves that. Our guest of honor reached that level several promotions ago.

• • •

Why did our guest of honor get this promotion? Because he deserves it. The rest of us have to keep telling ourselves that.

• • •

Our guest of honor started in the company as a nothing, and look at him now—a nothing with a fancy title.

. . .

What's amazing is that our guest of honor got this promotion so early—many, many years before he deserved it.

. . .

With this promotion, many of us will now be working for our guest of honor. The rest of us will continue to work against him.

. . .

I've been a close friend of our guest of honor for many years. Now that he's gotten this promotion I realize that I never really cared for him.

. . .

I'll say this about our guest of honor: this promotion hasn't gone to his head. I've worked with him for many years, and I can honestly say that not much has gone to his head.

. . .

Even though I thought I might get this promotion, I was hoping our guest of honor would get it. In fact, I hope he gets everything that's coming to him.

. . .

I must tell you that I came here tonight a little upset that I didn't get this promotion. But since I've let the air out of his tires in the parking lot, I feel much better.

. . .

So, our guest of honor has been promoted. I'll tell you how I feel about that. He's now just one other person I'll have to step over on my way to the top.

LEAVING THE COMPANY

He's the kind of guy who can brighten a room by leaving it.
—*Milton Berle*

Our guest of honor is leaving the company for something better, which has upset management. They didn't want the rest of us to know there was anything better.

. . .

Our guest of honor is leaving the company. We hated to lose him, but it was either that or pay him more money.

. . .

I cautioned our guest of honor to be careful about leaving the company. I reminded him the grass is always greener. And he told me, "It's not only greener, but I'm getting more of it."

. . .

Why is our guest of honor leaving the company? Well, he's following the advice of the great philosopher Yogi Berra, who said, "Whenever you come to a fork in the road, take it."

. . .

To me, going-away parties are sad—because they're always for somebody else.

. . .

Our guest of honor decided to stop working here. That was years ago. Now he's decided to leave the company.

. . . he's going to start not working somewhere else.

. . .

Our guest of honor is moving on to bigger and better things. At least, that's the story he bought.

. . .

I asked our guest of honor why he was leaving us. He said, "Like the three little pigs in the story, I'm going out to make my way in the world." It's comforting to know he's leaving with good, solid role models.

. . .

We wish our guest of honor well. But we want him to know that if he ever wants to return, we'll be here for him . . . because most of us can't get a better job like he can.

. . .

In sports, when an honored player leaves, they retire his jersey. We're going to do the next best thing. We're going to retire his desk chair.

. . . the wheels on it don't work anyway.

. . . come to think of it, that may be why he's leaving.

CONGRATULATIONS ON YOUR

RETIREMENT

Losing a Coworker

Around the House

Travel

Fishing

Golf

Gardening

A toast to your retirement:
    Remember when you have nothing to do,
    That no one does that better than you.

To your retirement:
    Gardening, reading, golf, and fishing,
    May you lead the life for which we've all been wishing.

To your retirement:
    Here's to doing nothing at all.
    Relax, enjoy, and just have a ball.

    When you're sitting at home with nothing to do,
    Think of us still at work. We're doing that too.

LOSING A COWORKER

I went to the doctor last week. He told me to take a hot bath before retiring. That's ridiculous. It'll be years before I retire.

—*Henny Youngman*

May your retirement plan be supervised by Jimmy Hoffa.

—*Steve Allen*

Retirement at sixty-five is ridiculous. When I was sixty-five, I still had pimples.   —*George Burns*

Our guest of honor is retiring. We won't see his smiling face around the office, listen to his pleasant laugh, or have him to chip in to solve a problem. On the other hand, I'd say now is a great time to buy stock in the company.

• • •

From what I can tell, our guest of honor retired from work several years ago. He's just now letting the company in on it.

• • •

Retirement: that's nature's way of telling you you're not getting any more paychecks.

. . .

I asked our retiree how long he's worked at this company. He said, "Oh, about half the years I've been here."

. . .

To all of our guest of honor's fellow employees, I say look at it this way: you're not losing a coworker; you're gaining a desk to rifle.

. . .

I asked our guest of honor, "What goes through your mind as you're about to retire?" He said, "Absolutely nothing. I don't want to start using my mind until I officially leave the company."

. . .

Retirement can be a happy time, a pleasant time, a joyous time, unless you're married to the retiree.

. . .

At the workplace I don't know what we'll do without our guest of honor. But you may have noticed, a lot of us didn't know what we were doing while he was there, either.

. . .

It's sad when you leave the workplace and go home, but look on the bright side. Chances are you'll get a better parking spot there.

. . .

Retirement is when you go home from work one day and never have to come back. The closest I can come to understanding that concept is one time, as a young lad, my father took me aside and left me there.

. . .

I knew one gentleman who had a very active and worthwhile retirement. I ran into him and his wife at a reunion once and I said to her, "How's your husband doing since he retired three years ago?" And she said, "He did?"

. . .

Retirement does not mean that the employee is no longer wanted or needed by the company. In this case, it happens to be true, but . . .

AROUND THE HOUSE

I'm an ordinary sort of fellow: 42 around the chest, 42 around the waist, 96 around the golf course, and a nuisance around the house.
—*Groucho Marx*

The trouble with not working is the minute you wake up in the morning, you're on the job.   —*Slappy White*

Our guest of honor says he's going to enjoy just staying around the house. That's good because he deserves the best. I just feel sorry for his spouse because she deserves better.

. . .

His wife's a little worried, but our guest of honor says, "Don't worry about me. I'll find things to do around the house." She says, "That's what I'm worried about."

. . .

His wife said she may find him part-time work. He says, "Why? I don't mind hanging around the house." She said, "I do."

. . .

Our guest of honor told the boss he plans to become a gentleman of leisure. And the boss said, "Become?"

. . .

He told me in retirement he plans to do absolutely nothing. I said, "How long can you do that?" He said, "Until I run out of things to do."

. . .

I think our guest of honor will be good at doing nothing around the house because when we had nothing to do at the office, we generally assigned it to him.

. . .

You may wonder how a person can be happy just doing nothing. Well, in our guest of honor's case, it's from years and years of practice.

. . .

His wife told me, "For the first week he's home I'll get him anything he wants. The second week I'll get him a job."

. . .

His wife said she'll be glad to have him home. She said, "For years he's been coming home and asking me what I did all day. Now he can stay home and watch me do it."

. . .

I think our guest of honor will be good at staying home and doing nothing. He almost had it down pat while he worked next to me.

. . .

I think our guest of honor will enjoy retirement. When you get up in the morning you've got nothing to do and all day to do it in.

. . . and I'll bet he'll still have trouble getting it done in time.

TRAVEL

I took the vacation I wanted all my life. I packed Alice and the kids and all the luggage in our station wagon and headed it right straight to Canada. Then I went to Las Vegas and had a ball.

—*George Gobel*

If you like to travel to out-of-the-way places where few people go, let your wife read the map. —*Norm Crosby*

When you look like your passport photo, it's time to go home.
—*Erma Bombeck*

I travel a lot. You know, I've been to almost as many places as my luggage has. —*Bob Hope*

Our guest of honor says he plans to go places now that he's retired. That's good because he certainly didn't go places while he worked here.

· · ·

You can tell from looking at our guest of honor that he's a traveling man. He must be. Practically everyone he meets tells him where to go.

· · ·

Puerto Vallarta, Mazatlán, Nairobi. Now that our guest of honor has the time, he plans to learn how to spell those places.

· · ·

Our guest of honor says that now that he's retired there'll be no grass growing under his feet. That either means he's going to travel or he plans to do his own gardening.

· · ·

He's going to visit the quiet, peaceful places of the world like Hawaii, Bermuda, the Bahamas. That makes sense. If he wanted to visit trouble spots he could just continue working here.

· · ·

Our guest of honor says he plans to live out of a suitcase from now on. That either means he's going to travel or he has to sell his house to augment his pension checks.

· · ·

I asked our guest of honor where he was going to travel—USA? UK? He said, "ANH." I said, "Where's ANH?" He said, "Anyplace not here."

· · ·

Our guest of honor said he's going to be busy because he's got places to go and people to see. Of course, while he worked here he had things to do, but that never kept him very busy.

· · ·

He plans to sit on a beach chair, just doing nothing. That's quite a change after years and years of sitting at a desk chair just doing nothing.

. . .

Our guest of honor is not a very sophisticated traveler. He looks forward to boarding an airplane for the food.

. . .

He's built for travel, you know. He has a seat bottom that can be used as a flotation device.

. . .

Our guest of honor said he plans to travel like the wind, which is typical of him—to use the cheapest mode of transportation.

 **FISHING**

My husband is one of those fishermen who wears those boots that extend up to the armpits so that when the water pours in, you are assured of drowning instantly. —*Erma Bombeck*

Our guest of honor says he is an incurable fisherman . . . unless, of course, he's lying about that, too.

. . .

Our guest of honor says he always catches his limit. I said, "How do you manage that?" He said, "Easy. I go where there's no fishing allowed."

. . .

Our guest of honor says that fishing is the most relaxing activity in the world. Those of us who have watched him at work find that hard to believe.

. . .

I asked him, "What's the hardest fish to catch?" He said, "One that keeps its mouth shut."

. . . he said that knowing I would be a speaker here tonight.

. . .

Our guest of honor said he enjoys fishing because it's a mental game. He likes to outsmart his prey. You have to admire a man who likes to prove he's smarter than a wall-eyed pike.

. . . some of the time.

. . .

I spend a lot of time fishing myself, but it's generally in conjunction with my golf game.

. . .

He said he generally throws the fish back. I said, "Why do you do that?" He said, "If you catch a 3-pound fish and take it home, it's a 3-pound fish. If you throw it back, when you get home it's a 5-pound fish."

. . .

I asked our guest of honor, "Where do you go to do most of your fishing?" He said, "Generally, near water."

. . .

I said, "Is anyone else in your family a fisherman?" He said, "No. Although several of them think they are."

. . .

Our guest of honor told me that to him fishing was the greatest sporting contest in the world. I asked why. He said, "Name one other sport where the loser is so delicious."

GOLF

Golf is a good walk spoiled.   —*Mark Twain*

Every time Jerry Ford plays golf, he gathers a big crowd. You know how people gather at the scene of an accident.   —*Bob Hope*

I found something that can take five points off your golf game—an eraser.   —*Joey Adams*

If you watch a game, it's fun. If you play it, it's recreation. If you work at it, it's golf.   —*Bob Hope*

I play in the low 80's. If it's any hotter than that, I won't play.
                                                     —*Joe E. Lewis*

Knowing our guest of honor, he'll probably go for several swims each day. Either that or he'll have to buy a new golf ball.

. . .

Our guest of honor likes to be alone in the woods, go places where few have gone before, and face challenges that are seemingly impossible. Unfortunately, he does all of this in a golf cart.

. . .

Our guest of honor will have a lot more time for golf—which is probably the only thing that will improve his swing.

. . .

One of his golfing goals is to shoot his age. And I hope he does it, too. I hope he's still playing golf when he's well over 100.

. . .

As one of his retirement gifts, we wanted to get him something he could use playing golf. But I understand he already has a calculator.

. . . some of those who have played with him suggested a lie detector.

. . .

Our guest of honor plays golf religiously. That means anytime he makes a good shot, it's considered a miracle.

. . .

He hits the ball all over the place. When he rents a golf cart, it has to be four-wheel drive.

. . .

Our guest of honor has fun playing golf. He says a great shot in golf is like your weekly salary. You don't have to earn it to enjoy it.

. . .

Our guest of honor is not a very good golfer. He's the guy who put the "P–U" in *Putt.*

. . .

Our guest of honor is going to enjoy golf in his retirement. I asked him earlier what his golf handicap was. He said, "Having to work for a living."

. . .

Our guest of honor has been trying to learn golf for a long time, but he confessed to me tonight that he's not very good at it. I said, "What kind of clubs do you use?" He said, "Clubs?"

Our guest of honor enjoys gardening, which has helped his career at work. He's used to spending a lot of time on his knees.

. . . and working around fertilizer.

. . .

He'll do a lot of gardening during his retirement. He says, "I plan to keep on gardening until the snails can outrun me."

. . .

Our guest of honor told me he plans to spend a lot of time in his garden. I don't know if that means he's going to work there or if his wife's going to take him outside and plant him.

. . .

Our guest of honor told me, "I'll be tossing fertilizer around and pruning all the dead wood I can find." It'll be just like he's back in management.

. . .

He said, "I like to work with dirt." I don't know what that says about those of us who have shared an office with him these past several years. . . .

. . .

I think our guest of honor will be very effective at gardening. I've worked with him many years and I know I wouldn't want to disagree with him while he had a Weedwacker in his hands.

. . .

He spends a lot of time on his hands and knees on the front lawn. We have a lot of people here who do that, but it's generally after one of these parties.

. . .

Our guest of honor says he loves to dig in the soil and get his hands dirty. I just mention that so those of you who shook hands with him earlier may want to wash up before dinner.

. . .

I think our guest of honor would be good at spreading fertilizer. Those of you who have heard him speak can probably vouch for that.

. . .

I said to our guest of honor, "When I see you a few months from now, may I ask 'How does your garden grow?' " He said, "Sure, if you'd like to get hit across the bridge of your nose with a hoe."

. . .

I said, "When I drive by your house in a few months will I see rows and rows of petunias, daffodils, and marigolds?" He said, "I hope not. I planted tomatoes."

WE ARE PLEASED TO INVITE YOU TO OUR

WEDDING ANNIVERSARY

So Many Years Together

Forgetting Anniversaries

Anniversary Gifts

Here's a toast to the many good times you've enjoyed together . . . and to the one or two that you just tolerated.

A toast to your anniversary. You've had many good years together, either that or one helluva good prenuptial agreement.

Here's to your love that has survived many years and is all the stronger for it.

A toast to your anniversary and the love that has held you together these many years:
When times are good, it's easy, brother.
When times are tough is when you need one another.

So MANY YEARS TOGETHER

It's nice to see such a happily married couple after so many years, because here's what "they" say about marriage:

It's better to have loved and lost than to have loved and married.
—*Sammy Shore*

Your wife is like TV. It's home and it's free. —*Slappy White*

Husbands are like fires. They go out if unattended.
—*Zsa Zsa Gabor*

My wife has a nice even disposition—miserable all the time.
—*Henny Youngman*

Twenty years ago, I married for richer, for poorer, for better, for worse. Fang's so lazy he hasn't been any of those things.
—*Phyllis Diller*

After all these years of marriage, I get the impression I married a knickknack. —*Phyllis Diller*

Many years ago, our guests of honor set sail on the sea of matrimony. And tonight, despite a few barnacles, they're still afloat.

. . .

Our guests of honor are celebrating their wedding anniversary tonight. I asked how many years it's been and they both answered, "Enough."

. . .

Our guests of honor told me that the secret of their longevity is that they never go to sleep angry at one another. Over their so many years of marriage, they figure they've lost about 8 years of sleep.

. . .

They've been together a long time. That's the nice thing about a big wedding. You feel obligated to stay together until it's paid for.

. . .

The groom told me he has the same thoughts tonight that he did on his wedding night. "Let's eat the cake; I'm starving."

. . .

She said, "It's our silver [golden] wedding anniversary. Let's go out and have an elegant, expensive, romantic dinner." He said, "OK, but I hope you're not going to expect this every 25 [50] years."

. . .

A couple of the groom's old girlfriends are here. At his age, what other kind of girlfriends would he have?

. . .

These two people were made for one another. Who else would have them?

. . .

It's nice to see a couple that's been married this long look so happy together. They're either doing something right or they have no idea that they're doing something wrong.

. . .

The groom told me that the suit he wore at his wedding fits him perfectly today. That gives you an idea how baggy it must have been on the day he was married.

· · ·

The groom told me he can still get into his wedding suit—about halfway.

· · ·

I asked the bride tonight, "Is he still the man you married?" She said, "He's almost double that."

· · ·

This couple should stay married a long time. The bride told me she married him for better, for worse, for richer, for poorer. And she's determined to stay with him till things start getting better and richer.

· · ·

Their wedding anniversary is proof that there is someone in this world for everybody. I just feel sorry for her that she had to get *him*.

. . . but somebody had to.

. . . just to take him out of circulation.

. . . and to make things safer for the rest of us.

· · ·

I said to someone earlier tonight, "They still make a beautiful couple, don't they?" He said, "Couple of what?"

· · ·

Our guests of honor have been married quite a while. There's some controversy over the number of years. Apparently, it's been longer for her than it has for him.

· · ·

They've been married a long time and it's nice to know that their love has grown even more than his waistline.

FORGETTING ANNIVERSARIES

I asked our guest of honor how many anniversaries he's forgotten over the years. He said, "I forget."

. . .

I have a friend who was married on February 29th so that he would only forget to buy an anniversary gift every four years.

. . .

Over the years he's forgotten a few anniversary gifts, but she gets even. She's forgotten to tell him which mushrooms are store-bought and which ones she picked herself.

. . .

I have a friend who tells me her husband has no idea what day they were married on. I said, "Oh, that's too bad." She said, "No, that's good. I can get an anniversary gift from him anytime I want one."

. . .

I asked our guest of honor if he was the kind to forget his anniversaries. He said, "Never more than once in the same year."

. . .

I spoke to our guest of honor earlier. I said, "You know what my mother used to say about people like you? 'You'd forget your head if it weren't screwed on.'" You know, he actually checked.

. . .

She told me that his forgetfulness helps keep the marriage going. Every time she's a little grumpy, he buys her flowers, takes her out to dinner, and wishes her a happy anniversary.

. . .

I asked him tonight, "When were you married?" He said, "I think it was in another life."

. . .

It seems only the men forget anniversaries. I asked the bride tonight and she told me, "I've never forgotten the day we were married. And heaven knows, there have been times when I've tried."

. . .

It is the secret to a long marriage. She told me tonight, she's going to keep him until he remembers an anniversary.

. . .

But he does buy lovely anniversary gifts, she told me. Fine china, elegant silverware, linen napkins. He once took her to a restaurant that uses those.

. . .

She has never forgotten an anniversary. As she told me, "If you were married to him, would you forget the day it happened?"

For our anniversary my wife wanted to go someplace she's never been before. So I took her to the kitchen.   —*Henny Youngman*

I don't know what to get my wife for our anniversary anymore. First she wanted a mink. I got her a mink. Then she wanted a silver fox. I got her a silver fox. It was ridiculous. The house was full of animals.
     —*Henny Youngman*

For our anniversary, my wife wanted a white mink coat. I told her I'd buy her a white mink coat when a man walked on the moon. My luck.   —*Henny Youngman*

She told me she has trouble getting him an anniversary gift. You know the dilemma: what do you get for a man who has everything? Her problem is: what do you get for the man who understands nothing?

· · ·

I asked her what she got her husband for their anniversary. She said, "Nothing. It's his favorite pastime."

· · ·

You know there are golf shops, tennis shops, and so on. I suggested she go to a store that specializes in his favorite activity. So she got him a gift certificate from Naps-R-Us.

· · ·

They already exchanged anniversary gifts. He gave her a piece of cheap jewelry; she gave him a piece of her mind.

· · ·

For their anniversary he bought something for the house—a round of drinks.

· · ·

She said she wanted something that a woman can use forever. He bought her a diet book.

· · ·

For her anniversary gift to him, she cooked his favorite meal. For his anniversary gift to her, he ate it.

· · ·

He said, "I'd like to have something that goes with my favorite sports coat." So she got him a clown's nose.

· · ·

For this anniversary they decided to get themselves something that they've both wanted since 1972. They bought a 1972 Cadillac.

· · ·

When they were discussing anniversary gifts, he said, "I've given you my undying love and devotion. What more could you want?" She came back with a list about 8 feet long.

· · ·

She told a friend, "I think I'll get something that's useful around the house." He overheard and thought she was seeing another man.

. . .

She asked if it was all right if she took the anniversary gift he gave her back to the store. She thought she could exchange it and maybe use the refund as a down payment on something worthwhile.

A PHOTO ALBUM OF MEMORIES
FOR YOUR

MARRIAGE

Wedding

Honeymoon

Marriage Lasts Forever

Here's to your wedding. May you always love each other a little bit more than yesterday but not quite as much as tomorrow.

A toast: May the bride and groom have as much happiness as I've had on several occasions. *—George Jessel*

To your wedding: Love not only makes the world go 'round, but it also makes the trip worthwhile.

To your wedding: May your love for each other grow as surely as your waistlines will.

My wife and I were happy for twenty years. Then we met.
—Rodney Dangerfield

My wife's an earth sign. I'm a water sign. Together we make mud.
—Rodney Dangerfield

We sleep in separate rooms, we have dinner apart, we take separate vacations. We're doing everything we can to keep our marriage together. *—Henny Youngman*

The first part of our marriage was very happy. But then, on the way back from the ceremony . . . *—Henny Youngman*

My parents want me to get married. They don't care who anymore, as long as he doesn't have a pierced ear, that's all they care about. I think men who have a pierced ear are better prepared for marriage. They've experienced pain and bought jewelry. *—Rita Rudner*

I found out after I got married that the husband's closet never comes with the apartment. —*Rodney Dangerfield*

Politics doesn't make strange bedfellows, marriage does.
—*Groucho Marx*

Since I've been married, I don't have to worry about bad breath. I never get a chance to open my mouth. —*Rodney Dangerfield*

If you want to read a book on love and marriage you've got to buy two separate books. —*Alan King*

Some stuff does bother me about being married . . . like having a husband. —*Roseanne Barr*

He tricked me into marrying him. He told me I was pregnant.
—*Carol Leifer*

A couple is driving to Miami Beach in a brand-new car. As they're driving, he puts his hand on her knee. She says, "We're married now, you can go a little farther." So he went to Fort Lauderdale.
—*Henny Youngman*

'Tis more blessed to give than receive; for example, wedding gifts.
—*H. L. Mencken*

I just found out why they rope off the aisles at a wedding. It's so the groom can't get away. —*Joey Adams*

I went to a wedding . . . I couldn't believe the groom was married in rented shoes. You're making a commitment for a lifetime, and your shoes have to be back by 5:30. —*Jerry Seinfeld*

I was the best man at the wedding. If I'm the best man, why is she marrying him? —*Jerry Seinfeld*

When a woman marries again it is because she detested her first husband. When a man marries again, it is because he adored his first wife. Women try their luck; men risk theirs. —*Oscar Wilde*

I wore a white dress on my wedding day . . . it had a big black hem.
—*Joan Rivers*

I was one of the few brides who ever got a request from the congregation to keep the veil on.   —*Phyllis Diller*

So, you two are going to tie the knot? Knowing him as well as I do, I'd suggest you tie it very tight.

. . .

You are going to accept him for richer, for poorer, for better, for worse. Take a good look at him and I think you can rule out a couple of those right from the start.

. . .

She has been looking for a good man for some time. And even though she is marrying *him*, I hope she doesn't abandon the search.

. . .

She's been going with him for quite a while, which is a good sign that she certainly knows how to handle children.

. . .

We're all so happy that you're having a big wedding. We're always happy when it means we get a free meal and a piece of cake.

. . .

I should warn you that he's very cheap. In fact, when you throw the bouquet, he may try to catch it.

. . . and sell it back to you.

. . .

I must say you do make a perfect couple . . . except for him.

. . .

He has so many faults, his nickname is San Andreas.

. . .

Let's put it this way, . . . I've known him a lot longer than you have, and I never offered to marry him.

. . . well, maybe I did, but that was at the bachelor party.

. . .

Soon you two will become one, which is about how many can survive on his salary.

. . . almost.

· · ·

And of course, being married now entitles you to do mother-in-law jokes, like these:

The only reason my mother-in-law wasn't on Noah's Ark was because they couldn't find another animal that looked like her.
—*Phyllis Diller*

The day I got married. What a day that was, when they said, "Speak now or forever hold your peace." Her family formed a double line.
—*Rodney Dangerfield*

I said to my mother-in-law, "My house is your house." So, she sold it.
—*Henny Youngman*

I'm just back from a pleasure trip. I took my mother-in-law to the airport.
—*Henny Youngman*

My mother-in-law had plastic surgery. She had a little work done on her nose . . . they put it in the middle of her face.
—*Redd Foxx*

My mother-in-law has such a big mouth. When she smiles, there's lipstick on her ears.
—*Redd Foxx*

HONEYMOON

A loser is a guy who goes on a honeymoon, and the motel employees toss a welcome-back party for his wife.
—*Charlie Manna*

We've been married for 50 years. Went back to the same hotel where we got married, had the same suite of rooms. Only this time I went into the bathroom and cried.   —*Henny Youngman*

On my honeymoon, Fang told me to unbutton my pajamas, and I wasn't wearing any.   —*Phyllis Diller*

The cooing stops with the honeymoon; the billing goes on forever.   —*Milton Berle*

After we made love he took a piece of chalk and made an outline of my body.   —*Joan Rivers*

Romeo and Juliet got married. They spent one night together and the next day he committed suicide. Then she committed suicide. I'm trying to figure what went on in that bedroom.   —*Alan King*

We don't know where they're going on their honeymoon. And probably when they get back, they won't remember where they've been.

. . .

We all know what a honeymoon is. It's a way of getting far away while someone else pays for the wedding.

. . .

Enjoy this, your first honeymoon. If you're like the rest of us, you'll never be able to afford a second one.

. . .

A honeymoon is when you go to a crowded resort so that you can have some time alone.

. . .

The secret of a good marriage is to make the honeymoon last forever, although it's hard to make reservations for that long.

. . .

A honeymoon is a week or two of complete togetherness. For many married couples, that's plenty.

. . .

I have a warning for you. You married each other for richer, for poorer. The poorer part comes when you get the bill for the honeymoon.

. . .

Remember this about your honeymoon. Two can live as cheaply as one, but not when you order room service.

. . .

You should try to make the honeymoon last forever . . . and you pretty much can if you pay for it in installments.

. . .

The honeymoon should be the happiest time of your life. And even if it isn't, they still charge you for it as if it were.

. . .

A honeymoon is a time when you can get away and leave all your troubles behind, except if the person you married is one of those troubles.

. . .

We wanted to have this celebration for you before your wedding and your honeymoon. Let's be sure to do this again on your 25th anniversary.

Anyone who thinks marriage is a fifty-fifty proposition doesn't understand either women or percentages. *—Henny Youngman*

Zsa Zsa Gabor has been married six times now; she's got rice marks on her face. *—Henny Youngman*

At least now he gives his wife something to live for: a divorce.
—*Henny Youngman*

Marriage is a great institution, but I'm not ready for an institution.
—*Mae West*

For the first four months of our marriage, I never took my wig off. Little did he know the hair he loved to touch he could take with him to the office.   —*Joan Rivers*

Last week I told my wife a man is like wine, he gets better with age. She locked me in the cellar.   —*Rodney Dangerfield*

Take a good look at the face of the mate you choose. You're going to wake up looking at that face for the rest of your life.

. . .

Marriage lasts forever. And those of us who are married will agree that at times it certainly seems that way.

. . .

Marriage is for a lifetime. Actually, it's for *two* lifetimes . . . served concurrently.

. . .

They really should hang a sign in all churches and wedding chapels that reads, "All decisions are final."

. . .

Our guests of honor should realize that when you purchase a marriage license it's a lifetime commitment. There should be no reason to save the receipt.

. . .

Marriage is forever . . . with time off for good behavior.

. . .

Matrimony is like getting a new car. Basically, you're buying your partner "as is."

And like it or not, you can get a lemon.

MANY HAPPY RETURNS
ON YOUR

BIRTHDAY

Getting Older

Old Age

We drink a toast to you on your birthday. It was either that or get a couple of Boy Scouts to help you across the street.

. . .

We drink to you on your birthday. You're not getting older, you're getting better . . . or vice versa.

. . .

A toast to your birthday. Another year older, another day wiser.

GETTING OLDER

You know you're getting older when you stoop down to tie your shoes and wonder what else you can do while you're down there.
—*George Burns*

He's a man who just reached middle age for the third time.
—*Joe E. Lewis*

You know you've reached middle age when someone tells you to pull in your stomach and you just did.   —*Milton Berle*

I don't plan to grow old gracefully. I plan to have face-lifts until my ears meet.   —*Rita Rudner*

Middle age is when you've met so many people that every new person you meet reminds you of someone else.   —*Ogden Nash*

There's an old saying, "You're not getting older; you're getting better." I used to believe that saying until I met our guest of honor.

. . . he's getting wider.

. . .

I guess you know you're getting older when you start to hurt in places where a few years ago you didn't even know you had places.

· · ·

You know you're getting older when the only parts of your body that don't hurt are the parts that have already fallen off.

· · ·

You know you're getting older when your favorite pickup line is, "Do you come here often, and do you know CPR?"

· · ·

Yep, you're only as young as you feel. And when you don't feel anything, you're old.

· · ·

You know you're getting older when everybody starts telling you how young you look.

· · ·

You know you're getting older when each time you want to stand up you have to think up a new sound to come out of your body.

· · ·

You know you're getting older when one of your favorite hobbies is liniment.

· · ·

You know you're getting older when even kids who aren't in the Boy Scouts start helping you across the street.

· · ·

You know you're getting older when people start talking to you louder than they talk to other people. I SAY, WHEN PEOPLE START TALKING TO YOU LOUDER THAN THEY TALK TO OTHER PEOPLE.

· · ·

You know you're getting older when all your favorite stories begin: "This was probably way before you were born, but . . ."

· · ·

You know you're getting older when your favorite form of recreation is just staying in whatever position you're already in.

OLD AGE

He's so old that when he orders a three-minute egg, they ask for the money up front. —*Milton Berle*

You're never too old to become younger. —*Mae West*

I don't fear old age. I am just becoming more aware of the fact that the only people who said old age was beautiful were usually 23-year-olds. —*Erma Bombeck*

My grandmother is over eighty and still doesn't need glasses. Drinks right out of the bottle. —*Henny Youngman*

She was so old, when she went to school they didn't have history. —*Rodney Dangerfield*

I have my eighty-seventh birthday coming up and people ask what I'd most appreciate getting. I'll tell you: a paternity suit. —*George Burns*

No woman should ever be quite accurate about her age. It looks so calculating. —*Oscar Wilde*

The secret to staying young is to live honestly, eat slowly, and lie about your age. —*Lucille Ball*

One should never trust a woman who tells one her real age. A woman who would tell one that, would tell one anything. —*Oscar Wilde*

Old age is when your eyes start to go, but it doesn't really matter because whatever you read today you're going to forget tomorrow anyway.

. . .

The best way to keep looking young is to hang around with older people.

. . . if you can find any.

. . .

Old age is when gravity is more than a law; it's an adversary.

. . .

Old age is when you can say anything you want at any time because hardly anybody listens to you anyway.

. . .

The strange thing about senility is that anybody who knows he has it doesn't have it.

. . .

If you get old enough, you don't have to act your age, because nobody knows what that age should act like.

. . .

Sure, it's nice to outlive all your enemies, but then again, you've got no one to gloat over.

. . .

You can get away with a lot in your old age. You can do things you've been dying to do since you were a kid.

. . .

After a certain age, there's one thing you learn never to say: "How do I look?"

. . . someone just might tell you.

. . .

We always say of the deceased that "they've gone on to a better place." But deep down inside, we're glad to still be here.

CONGRATULATIONS ON YOUR

NEW BABY

Having a Baby

Parenting

Here's a toast to your new baby . . . because nobody wants to give birth to an old baby.

A toast to your blessed event: For people your age, that means you're having a baby. For people my age, "blessed event" means you won the lottery.

A toast to your happiness: Soon the stork will be coming your way, followed shortly by the diaper service, the baby photographer, and probably an encyclopedia salesman or two.

HAVING
A
BABY

Did you hear the one about the expectant father who wanted to name the baby Oscar because it was his best performance of the year? —*Henny Youngman*

A little parenting advice: Don't call a baby-sitter who knows your children. She won't come. —*Phyllis Diller*

I once asked my father if things were bad for him during the Depression. He said the first six months were bad, then he got used to me. —*Rodney Dangerfield*

When I was pregnant, I told Fang the pains were three minutes apart. He used me to time the eggs. —*Phyllis Diller* ·

I was cesarean-born. You can't really tell. Although whenever I leave a house, I go out through a window. —*Steven Wright*

We delivered our child via natural childbirth. That's where it's be-lieved that women can counteract the incredible pain of childbirth through breathing. That's like asking a man to tolerate a vasectomy by hyperventilating. —*Dennis Wolfberg*

I want to have children, but my friends scare me. One of my friends told me she was in labor for thirty-six hours. I don't even want to do anything that feels good for thirty-six hours. —*Rita Rudner*

A woman came to ask the doctor if a woman should have children after thirty-five. I said thirty-five children is enough for any woman.
—*Gracie Allen*

I was born by C-section. This was the last time I had my mother's complete attention. —*Richard Jeni*

When my wife was about to give birth I said, "Honey, if it looks like you it would be great." She said, "If it looks like you, it'd be a miracle." —*Rodney Dangerfield*

A baby is an inestimable blessing and bother. —*Mark Twain*

I was an ugly baby. When my parents left me on a doorstep, they were arrested. Not for abandonment—for littering. —*Joan Rivers*

We haven't all the good fortune to be ladies. We have not all been generals, or poets, or statesmen, but when the toast works down to the babies we stand on common ground. We've all been babies.
—*Mark Twain*

Except that right side up is best, there is not much to learn about holding a baby. —*Heywood Broun*

The child had his mother's eyes, and his mother's nose, and his mother's mouth, which leaves his mother with a pretty blank expression. —*Robert Benchley*

My husband and I decided to explain the beautiful reproduction cycle to our kids through the animal kingdom. We bought two pairs of guppies and a small aquarium. We should have bought two pairs of guppies and a small reservoir. —*Erma Bombeck*

Congratulations on your blessed event. Take some advice from someone who's already been a parent. Get all your sleep in now.

· · ·

Babies are the greatest pleasure in the whole world, until you've had them a month or two. Then a good night's sleep is.

· · ·

Babies are a bundle of joy. It's just that seven or eight times a day you have to change the bundle.

· · ·

Hospitals treat expectant fathers like vice-presidents. They put you in a room someplace and forget about you.

· · ·

I told my wife, "I'd rather have the babies than do the grocery shopping." So we compromised. Now every time shopping day rolls around, I get morning sickness.

· · ·

I want you to take a look at our couple right now. That's the way they're going to be for a long time after this baby arrives—wide awake.

· · ·

When is the baby due? Well, as my grandmother used to say, "When the apple's ripe, it'll fall." Of course, if they go through all of this and wind up with an apple, it's going to be a terrible shock.

· · ·

So you're going to have a child, huh? Plan ahead. You've only got sixteen more years to use the car whenever you want to.

· · ·

I hope our guest of honor is smart enough to be a daddy. I asked him earlier if he wanted a boy or a girl. He said, "Yes."

· · ·

Newborn babies are precious. When you get that hospital bill you'll realize they work out to about $750 a pound.

· · ·

I'm sure you'll both enjoy this blessed event. Babies are cute and cuddly and precious. They're so much more fun than free time.

PARENTING

A little old lady was on a park bench. A neighbor admired her two little grandchildren and asked how old they were. The little old lady said: "The lawyer is four and the doctor is six."   —*Alan King*

As parents my wife and I have one thing in common. We're both afraid of children.   —*Bill Cosby*

My mother had a great deal of trouble with me, but I think she enjoyed it.   —*Mark Twain*

Mothers mold the children's mind. Some of you have done well. There are a lot of moldy-minded kids around.   —*Norm Crosby*

Parents were invented to make children happy by giving them something to ignore.   —*Ogden Nash*

The height of parental maturity is, of course, to learn to live with your child as he is—even if he is just like you.   —*Sam Levenson*

Babies on television never spit up on the Ultrasuede.
    —*Erma Bombeck*

Ah, the pitter-patter of little feet in the house. There's nothing like having a midget for a butler.   —*W. C. Fields*

I could now afford all the things I never had as a kid, if I didn't have kids.   —*Robert Orben*

Kids! I can't make them disappear, but I do wear dark glasses in the house hoping they won't recognize me.   —*Phyllis Diller*

Having a family is like having a bowling alley installed in your head.

—*Martin Mull*

Children have been known to take a few years off your life—like fifty or sixty.

—*George Burns*

The reason grandparents and grandchildren get along so well is that they have a common enemy.

—*Sam Levenson*

There are slight differences between mothers and grandmothers. Grandmothers say, "Stay in, it's cold outside." Mothers say, "Go out, it's good for you."

—*Erma Bombeck*

A grandfather is a man who can't understand how his idiot son had such brilliant children.

—*Milton Berle*

My grandmother was a very tough woman. She buried three husbands. Two of them were just napping.

—*Rita Rudner*

The only thing I ever said to my parents when I was a teenager was "Hang up. I got it."

—*Carol Leifer*

. . .

Parenting requires patience, endurance, forgiveness, understanding. And if the children aren't willing to do that, it's going to be tough.

. . .

No one can tell you how to be a good parent, except your children when they get to be teenagers.

. . .

You can take a test to see if you have the patience, flexibility, and endurance to be a good parent. You take this test when your child reaches the age of two.

. . .

I asked my mother what I should do to make sure that I raise my kids properly. She said, "I raised *you*. What do I know?"

. . .

You raise a child mostly by example. That's why to this day I still take a nap every day at two o'clock.

YOU ARE INVITED
TO BORROW THESE

INSULTS FOR ALL OCCASIONS

I drink to your charm, your beauty, and your brains—which gives you a rough idea of how hard up I am for a drink. —*Groucho Marx*

Let us toast the fools; but for them, the rest of us could not succeed.
—*Mark Twain*

I can't forget the first time I laid eyes on you . . . and don't think I haven't tried.
—*Henny Youngman*

You have a ready wit. Let me know when it's ready.
—*Henny Youngman*

I never forget a face, and in your case I'll remember both of them.
—*Henny Youngman*

There is a lot to say in her favor, but the other is more interesting.
—*Mark Twain*

You got a nice personality but not for a human being.
—*Jack E. Leonard*

His mother should have thrown him away and kept the stork.
—*Mae West*

I enjoyed talking to you. My mind needed a rest.
—*Henny Youngman*

What's on your mind, if you will allow the overstatement?
—*Fred Allen*

I never forget a face, but in your case I'll be glad to make an exception.
—*Groucho Marx*

Here's a toast that we may all learn to laugh at ourselves, because if we don't, someone else surely will.

• • •

Our guest of honor is a gem of a man. Of course, as you know, a gem is nothing more than a rock that got lucky.

• • •

Our guest of honor is a fine-looking gentleman. I'm sure most of us here wish that we could look that good when we get to be his age.

• • •

We have a rule at these affairs that if you can't say something nice about the guest of honor, don't say anything at all. This may be the first banquet done entirely in pantomime.

. . .

We have a rule at these affairs that if you can't say something nice about the guest of honor, don't say anything at all. So in conclusion . . .

. . .

I'd like to say that our guest of honor is probably the finest person I've ever met in my entire life. I'd like to say that, but I'd be laughed out of here if I did.

. . .

I'll tell you something about our guest of honor. Sometimes we say some nasty things at these roasts and the guest of honor's family gets annoyed. Tonight we said some nasty things about our guest of honor and his family just nodded in agreement.

. . .

All of us will agree that our guest of honor has a good head on his shoulders. Unfortunately, it's on his left shoulder instead of in the middle.

. . .

Our guest of honor is a very shy, reticent man. When we first told him about this affair, he said, "I don't think I'll be there." And we didn't care.

. . .

They don't make men like our guest of honor anymore. No, his sort went out of style years ago.

. . . he's like the Nehru jacket of personalities.

. . .

Our guest of honor is a self-made man. No professional would do the job.

. . .

Our guest of honor is living proof that having a goal, a dream, and struggling hard to attain it, don't always work.

. . .

Our guest of honor asked me earlier, "How are you going to introduce me?" I said, "Now, here's our guest of honor." He said, "Aren't you going to list all my accomplishments?" I said, "I just did."

. . .

Our guest of honor is a self-made man, and as you can tell, he found it difficult to get parts.

. . .

What can you say about our guest of honor that hasn't already been done to death in the Looney Tunes cartoons?

. . .

One thing you can certainly say about our guest of honor is that he's made something of himself. Of course, you can say the same thing about Lego building blocks.

. . .

Our guest of honor is a fine example to those young people who say, "I don't want to grow up. I don't want to mature. I don't want to get my head on straight." We can point to him and say right back to them, "If you don't, this is how you could turn out."

. . .

Our guest of honor is a humble man. He said to me earlier, "I don't want people reciting my accomplishments and glorifying my achievements—making me out to be some kind of hero." I assured him that all of our speakers have been told to stick with the truth.

. . . as painful as that may be to him.

. . . if he thought he was humble before, wait until after tonight.

. . .

When we kid at these affairs, we try to tell gentle jokes that don't come too close to a person's real shortcomings. In the case of tonight's guest of honor, it's hard to avoid.

Index